Y0-BSM-208

Who F*rted Now?

St. Martin's Press   NEW YORK

WHO F*RTED NOW? Copyright © 1990 by Philip Cammarata.
All rights reserved. Printed in the United States of America. No part of this book may be used or reproduced in any manner whatsoever without written permission except in the case of brief quotations embodied in critical articles or reviews. For information, address St. Martin's Press, 175 Fifth Avenue, New York, N.Y. 10010

Library of Congress Cataloging-in-Publication Data
Who f*rted now?
          p.   cm.
       ISBN 0-312-03952-2
       1. Flatulence—Humor.   2. Wit and humor. Pictorial.
    PN6231.F55W49   1990   89-24149
    818'.5402—dc20   CIP

First Edition

10 9 8 7 6 5 4 3 2 1

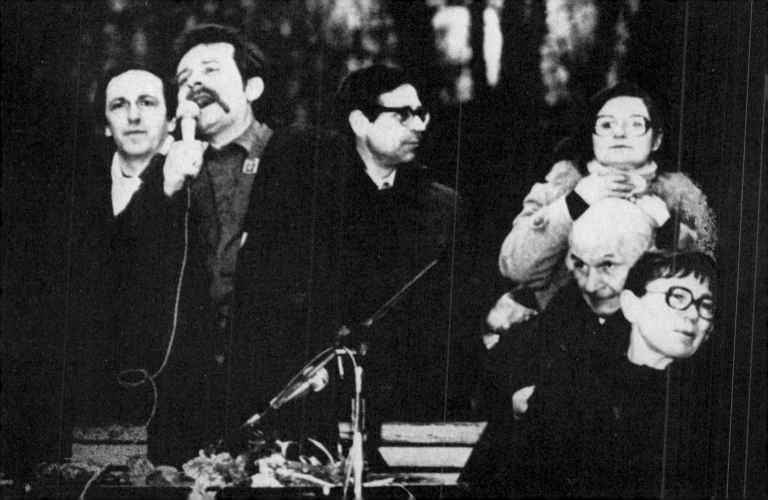

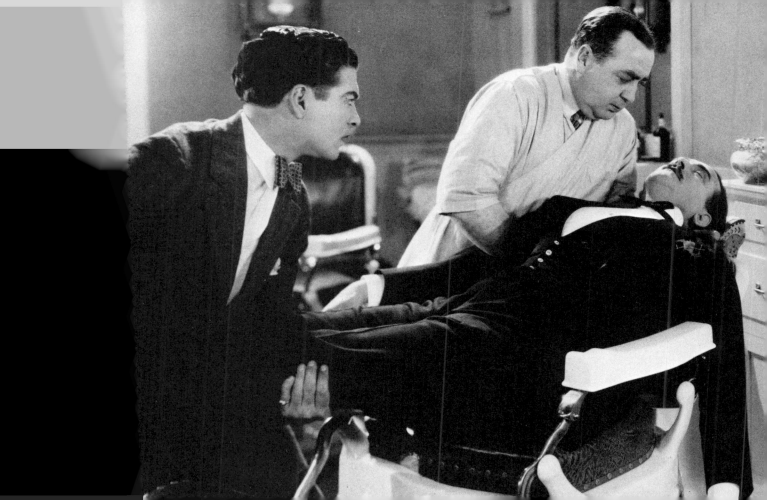

Photo Credits

1. UPI
2. Collection of Philip Cammarata
3. UPI
4. Collection of Philip Cammarata
5. Collection of Philip Cammarata
6. UPI
7. Collection of Philip Cammarata
8. UPI
9. Collection of Philip Cammarata
10. UPI
11. Collection of Philip Cammarata
12. AP
13. Collection of Philip Cammarata
14. AP
15. Collection of Philip Cammarata
16. Collection of Philip Cammarata
17. UPI
18. Collection of Philip Cammarata
19. UPI
20. Collection of Philip Cammarata
21. AP/Wide World Photos
22. Collection of Philip Cammarata
23. Collection of Philip Cammarata
24. UPI
25. UPI
26. UPI
27. New York Daily News
28. AP
29. Collection of Philip Cammarata
30. UPI

The Trip

NEW HAVEN UNIFIED SCHOOL DIST.
UNION CITY, CALIFORNIA

Y0-BSM-156

Written by Leya Roberts
Illustrated by Andy San Diego

"Ho hum," said Giraffe.

"Yes, ho hum," said Zebra.

3

"Let's take a trip," said Giraffe.

"Yes, let's take a trip," said Zebra.

4

Giraffe and Zebra ran across the grass.

Giraffe and Zebra ran across the rocks.

Giraffe and Zebra ran across the hills.

Giraffe and Zebra ran across the river.

Giraffe and Zebra ran across Lion's den.

"Yikes!" said Giraffe.

"Yikes!" said Zebra.

10

"ROAR!" said Lion.

Giraffe and Zebra zoomed across the river.

Giraffe and Zebra zoomed across the hills.

Giraffe and Zebra zoomed across the rocks.

Giraffe and Zebra zoomed across the grass.

"I love it here," said Giraffe.

"Yes, I love it here, too!" said Zebra.

16